21 Attributes that God will Reward

21
Attributes that God will Reward

Attracting divine reward through your lifestyle

Anthony Adefarakan

GLOEM, CANADA

CONTENTS

Dedication	1
Acknowledgement	2
Introduction	4
Attribute #1 — Loving Your Enemies	7
Attribute #2 — Praying in the Secret	10
Attribute #3 — Fasting Unnoticed	14
Attribute #4 — Secret Giving	19

CONTENTS

Attribute #5 | Diligently Seeking the Lord   22

Attribute #6 | Steadfast Service   25

Attribute #7 | Harvest of Souls   28

Attribute #8 | Time Investment   35

Attribute #9 | Sacrifice   38

Attribute #10 | Obedience and the Fear of God   41

Attribute #11 | Patience and Persistence   47

Attribute #12 | Hunger and Thirst for Righteousness   52

Attribute #13 | Faithfulness   55

Attribute #14 | Gratitude   59

CONTENTS

Attribute #15	Godly Jealousy	63
Attribute #16	Forgiving Others	66
Attribute #17	Humility and Meekness	70
Attribute #18	Holiness and Consecration	75
Attribute #19	Godly Marriage	78
Attribute #20	Righteous Living	81
Attribute #21	Persecution	83
	Conclusion	86
	WHY YOU REALLY NEED JESUS!	88
	PRAYER POINTS	93

CONTENTS

BECOME A FINANCIAL PARTNER WITH JESUS 94

About the Author 97

| 100

Dedication

I dedicate this book to God Almighty for His goodness and faithfulness in making His Word available to me. All glory to His Holy Name.

Also to everyone desirous of a vibrant walk with God, accessing divine rewards on a daily basis, I am in agreement with you all and I decree that grace for an effective walk with God is coming upon you in Jesus' Name.

Acknowledgement

I sincerely acknowledge my Eternal Father, Who alone is the Source of all wisdom. He is the Author and Finisher of my faith and it is of His fullness that the contents of this book have been drawn.

Also, I want to profoundly appreciate my dear parents – Prince and Mrs. Timothy Adefarakan – for bringing me up in the way of the Lord and for instilling righteousness consciousness in me. The wonderful education foundation I was given, coupled with their constant encouragement has empowered me to reach heights that were once beyond my imagination.

My most special appreciation goes to my sweetheart, Abisolami; without her help and support I would never have enjoyed the conducive atmosphere needed to publish this book. I appreciate your love, encouragement, and the support you give at all times. Thank you so much. I love you my Baby!

And to all my mentors in Ministry, I appreciate you all. Your investments in my life are not in vain. May the Lord reward you all in Jesus' Name.

Introduction

The principle of cause and effect cuts across the pages of scriptures. It is not unfamiliar to see expressions like **"If you obey, God will do this, but if you do not obey, God will do that."** There are always actions and reactions, causes and effects, decisions and consequences, deeds and repercussions etc.

The Bible presents God as a fair and just Judge Who rewards people according to what they do or refuse to do. Revelation 22:12 NKJV says *"And behold, I am coming quickly, and My reward is with Me, to give to every one according to his work."*

Also, Galatians 6:7 NKJV says *"Do not be deceived, God is not mocked; for whatever a man sows, that he will also reap."*

21 ATTRIBUTES THAT GOD WILL REWARD

When it comes to rewarding people, God is never partial; this is because He doesn't see as man sees (1 Samuel 16:7 NKJV), and He also knows all our motives for everything we do (Proverbs 16:2 NIV). So, for instance you may appear to everyone as a good person - may be through your philanthropic acts or something beneficial you do for people; but if your motives are impure, God will read them and reward you accordingly. He can't be fooled in anyway.

God is a just Rewarder; and in this book you will be introduced to Twenty-one (21) Attributes that He will reward in anyone's life. Now, there are countless attributes that will either attract God's reward or punishment; however, the focus of this book isn't on all. The purpose of this book is to reveal to you 21 Basic attributes that you can possess with the help of the Holy Spirit in order to enjoy God's rewards on a daily basis. And as you keep walking and fellowshipping with the Holy Spirit, He will flood your life with more of such attributes, thereby increasing your rewards.

Be blessed as you read on.

Anthony Adefarakan

Attribute #1

Loving Your Enemies

"...I say unto you, Love your enemies, bless them that curse you, do good to them that hate you, and pray for them which despitefully use you, and persecute you; That ye may be the children of your Father which is in heaven: for he maketh his sun to rise on the evil and on the good, and sendeth rain on the just and on the unjust. For if ye love them which love you, what reward have ye..." (Matthew 5:44-46 KJV)

Right from the time of Moses under the Old Covenant, the most reasonable reaction to one's enemies has always been to hate them and even find a way of destroying them if need be. That explains why we have expressions such as *'eye for eye, tooth for tooth, hand for hand, foot for foot, burn for burn, wound for wound, bruise for bruise'* under the Old Covenant (Exodus 21:24-25).

However, when Jesus Christ came on the scene to seal the New Covenant with His stainless Blood, He instituted a new order of grace of which loving our enemies is part. We are no longer to hate our enemies, rather we are to love them, bless them, feed them if they are hungry, pray for them and do good to them generally.

Now it is very important that we define who our enemies are at this juncture; in Jesus' context, our enemies are those who oppose our views and beliefs, those who frustrate our efforts, those who persecute us, those who spread false rumours about us, those who hate us and curse us, those who despitefully use us, those who seek our downfall, demotion and even destruction.

The dictionary actually describes an enemy as a person who is actively opposed or hostile to someone or something. The people in this category must be loved according to the teachings of Jesus.

What then does it mean to love our enemies?

Look at that Matthew 5:44-46 again; Jesus said we (as His followers) are to be good to them just as our Heavenly Father demonstrates His goodness to both the good and the evil in causing the rain to fall and causing the sun to rise for both of them.

He also went further to say that it is loving our enemies and not those who love us that attracts divine reward.

So, to attract divine reward in this area, stop fighting with those who strongly oppose you and start doing what Proverbs 25:21-22 NLT says;

"If your enemies are hungry, give them food to eat. If they are thirsty, give them water to drink. You will heap burning coals of shame on their heads, and the LORD will reward you."

May the grace to do this come upon you mightily in Jesus' Name.

Attribute #2

Praying in the Secret

"...when thou prayest, thou shalt not be as the hypocrites are: for they love to pray standing in the synagogues and in the corners of the streets, that they may be seen of men. Verily I say unto you, They have their reward. But thou, when thou prayest, enter into thy closet, and when thou hast shut thy door, pray to thy Father which is in secret; and thy Father which seeth in secret shall reward thee openly..." (Matthew 6:5-6 KJV)

The subject of prayer is a very vital part of the Christian faith because it is humanity's means of communication with divinity. When you pray, you are talking to God; and Jesus (Who actually came from the One you are praying to) gave some specific instructions worth paying attention to if your prayers must attract divine response.

Let's take a closer look at that Matthew 6:5-6;

Firstly, it says *'when thou prayest'*.

By this, Jesus was signifying that prayers should not be a matter of *'if'* but *'when'*. As a believer, prayer is to your spirit-man what oxygen is to your body. If your prayer life is dependent on certain conditions like if you feel like, if there is time, if you wake up, if you are not tired, if there is a Public Holiday, if your children are not around, if you feel happy, if there is a church program, among other conditions, you will dry up spiritually; it's just a matter of time.

'When' means it should be part of your schedule. *'When'* indicates an adverb of time: like in the morning, in the evening, at noon, now, today, tomorrow, at midnight etc. Jesus expects us to pray without ceasing (1 Thessalonians 5:17); so our prayer life MUST never be dependent on any con-

ditions just as breathing cannot be subject to any condition.

That being said, Jesus described certain forms of prayer as hypocritical. Prayers that are targeted towards attracting the attention of others for any form of encomiums or accolades attract no further rewards from God apart from the attention they already got from others.

If the aim of your prayer is to stage a show business so others watching can praise you for your piety, eloquence, grammatical construction, uncommon prayer posture or extended length of prayer time, you have nothing to expect from God as far as reward is concerned.

To attract divine reward however, Jesus said you should go into your closet (out of public view) and pray to your Father in the secret so that He can reward you openly.

It is the open reward that God gives in response to your secret prayers that will make others know that you have a vibrant prayer life, not the grammar they hear you chant in public show prayers.

Now, does that mean we should never pray in the public? No, Jesus never said that. He was basically addressing the hypocrisy element in such prayers: ***'that they may be seen of men'.*** The motive of such prayers isn't to secure God's attention, rather it is to attract human praise.

Pay attention to your prayer life; are you getting the right rewards?

Attribute #3

Fasting Unnoticed

"Moreover when ye fast, be not, as the hypocrites, of a sad countenance: for they disfigure their faces, that they may appear unto men to fast. Verily I say unto you, They have their reward. But thou, when thou fastest, anoint thine head, and wash thy face; That thou appear not unto men to fast, but unto thy Father which is in secret: and thy Father, which seeth in secret, shall reward thee openly." (Matthew 6:16-18 KJV)

This is very similar to the charge Jesus gave when addressing the issue of prayer. Fasting, which connotes self-denial of food, comfort or other pleasures for the purpose of seeking the face of God or obtaining certain results in prayer, should not be done as show-business.

Take note He also said *'when ye fast'* not *'if ye fast'*. So, fasting should be a part of our lives.

Now how are we not to fast? According to Jesus, we are not to fast as the hypocrites do. We are not to look so sad, disfigured with drooping faces so everyone around us can know that we are fasting. If we do that, our reward is the attention we get from others.

How then are we expected to fast?
When you are fasting, take your bath, cream your body and hair, look good and smart, dress properly and don't go about talking as if you are being punished. Leave no sign for anyone to discover you are fasting; let your fasting be seen only by God and He will reward you openly.

Look at what Isaiah 58 also has to say about this subject matter.
It says in verses 1-7:
"Shout with the voice of a trumpet blast. Shout aloud! Don't be timid.

Tell my people Israel of their sins! Yet they act so pious!

They come to the Temple every day and seem delighted to learn all about me.

They act like a righteous nation that would never abandon the laws of its God.

They ask me to take action on their behalf, pretending they want to be near me.

'We have fasted before you!' they say. 'Why aren't you impressed?

We have been very hard on ourselves, and you don't even notice it!'

"I will tell you why!" I respond. "It's because you are fasting to please yourselves.

Even while you fast, you keep oppressing your workers.

What good is fasting when you keep on fighting and quarreling?

This kind of fasting will never get you anywhere with me.

You humble yourselves by going through the motions of penance,

bowing your heads like reeds bending in the wind.

21 ATTRIBUTES THAT GOD WILL REWARD

You dress in burlap and cover yourselves with ashes.

Is this what you call fasting? Do you really think this will please the LORD?

"No, this is the kind of fasting I want: Free those who are wrongly imprisoned;

lighten the burden of those who work for you.

Let the oppressed go free, and remove the chains that bind people.

Share your food with the hungry, and give shelter to the homeless.

Give clothes to those who need them, and do not hide from relatives who need your help."

That's what God wants from you when you fast. And if you do, you can expect His rewards as mentioned in verses 8 - 12 of the same chapter.

"Then your salvation will come like the dawn, and your wounds will quickly heal.

Your godliness will lead you forward, and the glory of the LORD will protect you from behind.

Then when you call, the LORD will answer. 'Yes, I am here,' he will quickly reply

...Then your light will shine out from the darkness,

and the darkness around you will be as bright as noon.

The LORD will guide you continually, giving you water when you are dry

and restoring your strength.

You will be like a well-watered garden, like an ever-flowing spring.

Some of you will rebuild the deserted ruins of your cities.

Then you will be known as a rebuilder of walls and a restorer of homes."

Fast the way God wants and your reward shall be great.

Attribute #4

Secret Giving

"Take heed that ye do not your alms before men, to be seen of them: otherwise ye have no reward of your Father which is in heaven.

Therefore when thou doest thine alms, do not sound a trumpet before thee, as the hypocrites do in the synagogues and in the streets, that they may have glory of men. Verily I say unto you, They have their reward. But when thou doest alms, let not thy left hand know what thy right hand doeth: That thine alms may be in secret: and thy Father which seeth in secret himself shall reward thee openly." (Matthew 6:1-4 KJV)

Alms refers to money, food or other materials (items) donated to relief the poor; an act of charity. These can either be given to the poor directly or donated through agencies involved in catering for the poor.

Now as laudable as this act is, Jesus taught that it could go unrewarded by God.

Jesus warned that almsgiving should not be done in order to attract attention or praise to ourselves. He said it shouldn't be done with the motive of being seen by men; attracting the attention of media to broadcast what we are doing, making mention of it so people could think of us as generous; otherwise there won't be any reward from God.

Rather, when you give alms, He said, your left hand should not even know what your right hand is doing. It should be done in secret, confidentially and if possible in anonymity; so that the Almighty God Who sees what is done in the secret may reward you openly.

Charitable acts that will attract divine reward

must be done to God's glory; and not to attract the praise of men.

Luke 6:38 NIV says *"Give, and it will be given to you. A good measure, pressed down, shaken together and running over, will be poured into your lap. For with the measure you use, it will be measured to you."*

For this promised reward to be yours, start giving the way Jesus taught.

Attribute #5

Diligently Seeking the Lord

"But without faith it is impossible to please Him, for he who comes to God must believe that He is, and that He is a rewarder of those who diligently seek Him." (Hebrews 11:6 NKJV)

The Bible says God is a Spirit and He constantly seeks those who will worship Him in spirit and in truth (John 4:23-24).

To relate with God, you must necessarily believe that He exists, even though you can't see Him. That's where faith comes in. Hebrews 11:1 describes faith as the substance of things hoped for, the evidence of things not seen.

You must believe everything about God – His Personality, His Power, His Plans and Purposes, His Judgments, His Decisions, His Instructions, His Promises, His Prophecies among other things that make Him Who He is.

To believe all these things, they first have to be discovered. And He is the One Who reveals them according to Deuteronomy 29:29. So you will have to seek Him diligently through prayers, studies, fellowship, obedience etc.

As you begin to seek Him this way, you will start attracting the rewards that go with seeking the Lord. And one of those rewards is abundance of revelation. He will start revealing things to you.

Note however that the Lord doesn't just reward those who seek Him; rather He rewards those who seek Him DILIGENTLY. So, you don't want to be lazy or lackadaisical in your pursuit of God. Anything you do for the Lord must be done diligently –pray diligently, preach diligently, serve diligently, give diligently etc. God is a Rewarder of those who diligently seek Him.

Attribute #6

Steadfast Service

"Therefore, my beloved brethren, be steadfast, immovable, always abounding in the work of the Lord, knowing that your labor is not in vain in the Lord." (1 Corinthians 15:58 NKJV)

God will never owe any man. There is nothing you are doing for the Lord that will be in vain. Just because certain expectations are not being met in your life at the moment doesn't mean your services are in vain. God takes note of everything that is done to His glory. He sees your intercessory prayers, your labour in the Word, your evangelistic efforts, your almsgiving, your faithfulness among all other things you do for the benefit and expansion of His Kingdom. Not one of those services escapes His attention and He will definitely reward you for every one of them.

Did you know there are some things you do for the Lord and don't remember? Yes, there are. But He never forgets any.

Look at Matthew 25:31-40 NLT:

"But when the Son of Man comes in his glory, and all the angels with him, then he will sit upon his glorious throne. All the nation will be gathered in his presence, and he will separate the people as a shepherd separates the sheep from the goats. He will place the sheep at his right hand and the goats at his left.

"Then the King will say to those on his right, 'Come, you who are blessed by my Father, inherit the Kingdom prepared for you from the creation of the world. For I was hungry, and you fed me. I was thirsty, and you gave me a drink. I was a stranger, and you invited me into your home. I was naked, and you gave me clothing. I was sick, and you cared for me. I was in prison, and you visited me.'

"Then these righteous ones will reply, 'Lord,

when did we ever see you hungry and feed you? Or thirsty and give you something to drink? Or a stranger and show you hospitality? Or naked and give you clothing? When did we ever see you sick or in prison and visit you?'

"And the King will say, 'I tell you the truth, when you did it to one of the least of these my brothers and sisters, you were doing it to me!"

Do not be discouraged at any point in time; keep serving the Lord steadfastly in any capacity He has called you to serve; keep loading your cloud; your reward is coming soon.

Revelation 22:12 NKJV says *"And behold, I am coming quickly, and My reward is with Me, to give to every one according to his work."*

Attribute #7

Harvest of Souls

"Even now the harvest workers are receiving their reward by gathering a harvest that brings eternal life. Then everyone who planted the seed and everyone who harvests the crop will celebrate together." (John 4:36 CEV)

"You did not choose me; I chose you and appointed you to go and bear much fruit, the kind of fruit that endures. And so the Father will give you whatever you ask of him in my name." (John 15:16 GNT)

Bearing fruits is very important to God. As a matter of fact, the very first thing He said to Adam and Eve after creating and blessing them was to be fruitful. He doesn't joke with fruits; especially eternal fruits – souls.

In Matthew 28:18-20, Jesus said *"...All power is given unto me in heaven and in earth. Go ye therefore, and teach all nations, baptizing them in the name of the Father, and of the Son, and of the Holy Ghost: Teaching them to observe all things whatsoever I have commanded you: and, lo, I am with you alway, even unto the end of the world. Amen."*

That's what is popularly referred to as the Great Commission.

As God's children, we have been appointed to go and win souls into His Kingdom. We are to announce that Jesus saves, heals, delivers and sets free. That is one task the Lord has committed into the hands of His followers. And there are both earthly and heavenly rewards for doing so. For instance, according to the John 15:16 quoted above, as a soul winner, you get whatever you ask God for. Through the Name of Jesus, you no longer get to have unanswered prayers.

Now, many religious denominations have complicated this Great Commission and a lot of believers are finding it so difficult to carry out. But here are some revelations on how you can be an effective soul winner wherever you find yourself through the Help of the Holy Spirit. Read the articles below for enlightenment on this subject matter: ***His Witnesses Part 1 and 2.***

His Witnesses Part 1: Acts 1:8

The Lord Jesus said His followers (believers) would be His witnesses from their immediate environment to the uttermost part of the earth – all by the ability and power the Holy Spirit supplies (Acts 1:8).

Though that doesn't sound like a difficult task, yet many of us believers are finding it difficult to carry out partly due to the kind of teachings/methods we have been previously exposed to. Some of us have been taught that in order to evangelize, we must load up our heads with many Bible verses; go from house to house knocking on peoples' doors or preach so convincingly in order to win someone over.

Well, there is nothing wrong in doing any of those things; but my Master said you shall be His witnesses.

Who then is a witness?

A witness is one who gives a testimony based on what he/she has experienced or knows about a person or an event. Acts 22:15 says "For thou shall be His witness unto all men of what thou hast seen and heard".

To evangelize then simply means telling all men that Jesus is the Way to the Father and that He is the ONLY Saviour from sin and eternal death (John 14:6).You are also to support this claim by telling them what you have seen and heard about Jesus.

At least you have heard that He heals all sicknesses, He forgives sins, He delivers from all kinds of oppression or you most probably have seen some of His Mighty works in your own very life. Those are the things He wants you to tell others. You don't have to convince anybody.

When a witness is called into the box in a law court, he is only asked to say all he knows about the case at hand. Nobody ever asks a witness to convince the court whether a case is true or false. Convincing is the work of the lawyer and Jesus is our Mediator and Advocate Who does the convincing through His Holy Spirit (1 John 2:1, John 16:13).

However, note that the Master only said "Go ye..." in the Great Commission according to Matthew 28:18-20; He didn't specify "How" you are to go. This will be considered in the Part 2 of this piece. Once you are saved, you have a standing order to tell others about the One Who saved you. Arise and get into the witnessing business, the reward is so handsome. Shalom!

His Witnesses Part 2: Matthew 28:18-20

From "His Witnesses Part 1", we discovered that the Lord Jesus Christ only wants us as believers to be His witnesses to the whole world of the things which we have seen and heard about Him by the power of the Holy Spirit (Acts 1:8, Acts 22:15). And that is to continue until the whole world is reached and then the end will come (Matt 24:14).

Now, how are we to go about this?

It's very simple. Get baptized in the Holy Ghost

(Luke 11:13) and "Go ye into the world" with the gospel as Christ's witness by doing any of the following:

Write it – as tracts, books, pamphlets, letters, bulletins, cards etc

Wear it – print the message on shirts, caps, tags, wrist bands, and wear them. Also print on windscreens, doorposts etc

Share it – in meetings, discussions, trainings, workshops etc

Air it – on Radios, Television, Cable Channels etc

Post it – on Facebook, Twitter, Instagram, Blogsites, and on the internet generally.

Drive/Sponsor it – form an evangelical group, join an existing group, promote or fund the activities of soul winners' group (missions).

Sing it – compose songs, wax albums, do soundtracks, callertunes etc

Organize/Arrange it – through luncheons, tourism, cruises, trips, parties, seminars etc

Act it – through drama, road shows, film shows, cinemas etc

Pray it – by interceding for sinners' salvation, asking God to send more laborers into His harvest

(Matt 9:37-38)

Live it – by your lifestyle, dispositions, behavior (Acts 11:26; 4:13)

Preach it – verbally either publicly or privately, in houses, streets, shops. Also to individuals or groups of people.

By all means, just keep witnessing.

JESUS IS THE BEST PRODUCT ANYONE CAN MARKET, AND THE REWARDS ARE SO ATTRACTIVE!

Attribute #8

Time Investment

"But seek ye first the kingdom of God, and his righteousness; and all these things shall be added unto you." (Matthew 6:33 KJV)

The Kingdom of God refers to God's will and purpose, which includes the salvation of sinners, healing of sicknesses, deliverance from all manners of oppression and satanic influences, sight to the blind, speech to the dumb, hearing to the deaf, walking to the lame, fruitfulness to the barren, becoming like Christ through the power of His Spirit and the Word, knowledge of the truth to the spiritually ignorant, redemption of nations among His other beautiful restoration plans.

When you make such matters that are so important to God your priority, and you do whatever He asks you to do concerning them, you are seeking first His kingdom and His righteousness. And the reward is contained right in that same verse, all these things (that people are running after, borrowing to buy, begging to possess) will be ADDED unto you (without struggles).

Isn't that a great reward? But you've got to make His priority your own priority as well. That's what He demands of you.

If you however decide to go about your own activities and plans without any regard for what He wants, then you will have to keep on struggling because He won't add it to you. You don't want to finish listening to the early morning news, take coffee, go to work, speak with friends over the phone, go watch some games, grab some dinner and hit the sofa before saying your first prayer for the day. That's seeking His kingdom last, not first. Or you collect your paycheck, allocate funds to different channels and when everything else has been taken care of, you now give Him some of the left overs as offering. That's not how to make Him your priority. You want to honour Him with the first part of your income before you begin spending the rest. That's how to make Him first in your life.

Get this, the God of Heaven is a big Rewarder of those who invest the choicest part of their time in His Kingdom affairs. Everyone who gives their time to serve Him, praise Him, preach His Gospel among other Kingdom tasks can be sure to expect His handsome rewards in this life and in the one to come.

The time you commit to the things of God is never spent or wasted; rather it's a profitable investment in the Kingdom.

Attribute #9

Sacrifice

"Then Peter spoke up. "Look," he said, "we have left everything and followed you. What will we have?"

Jesus said to them, "You can be sure that...everyone who has left houses or brothers or sisters or father or mother or children or fields for my sake, will receive a hundred times more and will be given eternal life." (Matthew 19:27-29 GNT)

Profitability has always been the primary focus of every business transaction. No one in their right senses will know in advance that losses are inevitable in a business deal and still go ahead with it.

Now, this is not only true in the world of business and investments, it is equally an established

21 ATTRIBUTES THAT GOD WILL REWARD

fact in God's kingdom – where all Christians belong.

Jesus had called and chosen His disciples and engaged them in various ministerial tasks; however, a time came when Peter (one of His disciples) spoke up and asked Jesus a direct question as quoted in Matthew 19:27 above. He said '...*we have left everything and followed you. What will we have?*'

You see, Peter was a fisherman by profession before he became a disciple of Jesus, and he knew how senseless it would be to go out fishing all day without any plan put in place to catch some fish for consumption and probably sale – which represent the reward of the fishing labour.

So, he wanted to be sure he wasn't just wasting his time by following Jesus. He wanted Jesus to assure him and by extension others that following Him was a profitable venture.

Now, it is important to note that Jesus didn't

rebuke him for asking; rather He answered him and gave him all the assurance he needed to prove to him that following Him has great rewards.

What Jesus told Peter then He is telling us now; there is nothing you sacrifice for His sake that will not be rewarded in hundred folds. Your sacrifice of time, money, comfort, food, clothes, shelter, career, being away from family members for the sake of His work will all be rewarded in this life and also in eternity.

Don't be weary in all your sacrificial commitments towards establishing God's kingdom on earth, great are your rewards.

Attribute #10

Obedience and the Fear of God

"Now it shall come to pass, if you diligently obey the voice of the Lord your God, to observe carefully all His commandments which I command you today, that the Lord your God will set you high above all nations of the earth. And all these blessings shall come upon you and overtake you, because you obey the voice of the Lord your God." (Deuteronomy 28:1-2 NKJV)

"And the king of Egypt spake to the Hebrew midwives, of which the name of the one was Shiphrah, and the name of the other Puah: And he said, When ye do the office of a midwife to the Hebrew women, and see them upon the stools; if it be a son, then ye

shall kill him: but if it be a daughter, then she shall live. But the midwives feared God, and did not as the king of Egypt commanded them, but saved the men children alive...Therefore God dealt well with the midwives: and the people multiplied, and waxed very mighty. - And it came to pass, because the midwives feared God, that he made them houses." (Exodus 1:15-21 KJV)

Firstly, let's consider the obedience part according to Deuteronomy 28:1-2. It says if you diligently obey the voice of the Lord, to observe carefully His commands in order to carry them out, certain blessings (rewards) will become yours.

What are the rewards? God will set you high above all the nations of the earth.

Is that all? Not at all; look at additional rewards in verses 3-13 of the same chapter according to the New Living Translation:

"Your towns and your fields will be blessed. Your children and your crops will be blessed.

The offspring of your herds and flocks will be

blessed. Your fruit baskets and breadboards will be blessed. Wherever you go and whatever you do, you will be blessed.

"The LORD will conquer your enemies when they attack you. They will attack you from one direction, but they will scatter from you in seven!

"The LORD will guarantee a blessing on everything you do and will fill your storehouses with grain. The LORD your God will bless you in the land he is giving you.

"If you obey the commands of the LORD your God and walk in his ways, the LORD will establish you as his holy people as he swore he would do. Then all the nations of the world will see that you are a people claimed by the LORD, and they will stand in awe of you.

"The LORD will give you prosperity in the land he swore to your ancestors to give you, blessing you with many children, numerous livestock, and abundant crops. The LORD will send rain at the proper time from his rich treasury in the heavens and will bless all the work you do. You will lend to many nations, but you will never need to borrow from them. If you listen to these commands of the LORD

your God that I am giving you today, and if you carefully obey them, the LORD will make you the head and not the tail, and you will always be on top and never at the bottom."

Those are great blessings guaranteed by the Lord Himself and all He requires of you is just to live a life of obedience. That's all! May the grace to live this life of absolute obedience to God come upon you in Jesus' Name. And may all these blessings also find expression in your life in Jesus' Name.

Now to the second part, the Fear of God. It is the foundation upon which obedience is built. If you don't have the fear of God, you won't regard Him let alone obey Him.

And when it comes to obeying men (authorities especially) or obeying God, you must always choose to obey God. Isaiah 8:13 NIV says *"The LORD Almighty is the one you are to regard as holy, he is the one you are to fear, he is the one you are to dread."*

Those two midwives in the Exodus 1:15-21 quoted above chose to fear God rather than the king of Egypt and did not commit the sin the king had asked them to commit. As a result of their demonstration of the fear of God, He treated them well and gave them children of their own.

Develop the fear of God and you will no longer find it difficult to obey God. And as you keep obeying Him, the rewards will start flowing towards you.

Take note of this as well, you don't always get to understand everything before you obey. God may not share the entire scope of things with you before He requires your obedience. Remember the Wedding in Cana of Galilee where Jesus turned water to wine? The story is in John 2:1-11. Before the miracle happened, Mary had already told the wine servers, *'Whatever He asks you to do, do it'*.

And what did Jesus do? He asked the servers to do something everyone would call stupid considering the need at hand at that moment. But the servers foolishly filled the pots with water as instructed, and wine came out of that obedience.

Do you need some miracles? Talk to the God of miracles, and whatever He asks you to do, just do it. That's living a life of obedience.

Attribute #11

Patience and Persistence

"But let patience have its perfect work, that you may be perfect and complete, lacking nothing." (James 1:4 NKJV)

"But the God of all grace, who hath called us unto his eternal glory by Christ Jesus, after that ye have suffered a while, make you perfect, stablish, strengthen, settle you." (1 Peter 5:10 KJV)

Patience has been defined as the capacity to accept or tolerate delay, trouble, or suffering without getting angry or upset while persistence means continuing firmly or obstinately in a course of action in spite of difficulty or opposition.

These are great virtues that attract handsome rewards from God every time they are exhibited. As a matter of fact, there is no way you will be able to relate with God without patience and persistence because His ways are not your ways (Isaiah 55:8-9).

The people who walked with God in times past were people of patience, and God rewarded them for it.

Consider Abraham and Sarah who waited for 25 years before they got the promise of Isaac fulfilled to them, and Job who also remained patient during his life threatening ordeal until his restoration came.

Hebrews 10:36 KJV says *"...ye have need of patience, that, after ye have done the will of God, ye might receive the promise."*

Now it is very important to let you know that patience doesn't just come upon anyone, it is not a gift; rather it is a fruit that has to be cultivated. You develop patience, that's how you get it. And this development doesn't happen when things are going your way, when you are victorious, when you are successful or when everything looks good. Patience is developed in the furnace of affliction, adversity, frustration, delay, misfortune, failure, losses among other circumstances one would ordinarily described as unfortunate.

So when you pray for something to happen and that thing is not happening, it's possible you have just been served a notice for patience development. Every trial of faith has one purpose – to develop your patience. And if you choose to grow through each one, you will become perfect, strengthened and settled in every area of life as promised in 1 Peter 5:10.

James 1:2-4 NKJV says *"My brethren, count it all joy when you fall into various trials, knowing that the testing of your faith produces patience. But let patience have its perfect work, that you may be perfect and complete, lacking nothing."*

Persistence works just the same way. You keep at it until you get your desired results despite oppositions and obstacles.

Jesus gave a parable in Luke 18:1-8 KJV to encourage persistence especially in prayer.

"And he spake a parable unto them to this end, that men ought always to pray, and not to faint; Saying, There was in a city a judge, which feared not God, neither regarded man: And there was a widow in that city; and she came unto him, saying, Avenge me of mine adversary. And he would not for a while: but afterward he said within himself, Though I fear not God, nor regard man; Yet because this widow troubleth me, I will avenge her, lest by her continual coming she weary me. And the Lord said, Hear what the unjust judge saith. And shall not God avenge his own elect, which cry day and night unto him, though he bear long with them? I tell you that he will avenge them speedily. Nevertheless when the Son of man cometh, shall he find faith on the earth?"

From that parable it becomes clear that you will

eventually get what you want if you refuse to give up. God rewards persistence as well as patience. So, cultivate them and let them reflect in your attitude towards life and situations on a daily basis.

Attribute #12

Hunger and Thirst for Righteousness

"Blessed are those who hunger and thirst for righteousness, for they will be filled." (Matthew 5:6 CSB)

The Word of God says every one that seeks finds (Matthew 7:8); so if your hunger and thirst are for righteousness, Jesus promised you will be filled.

Now, to hunger and thirst for righteousness isn't just about wishing to live holy or obey God. It is rather a panting that is geared towards knowing the will of God with full readiness to carry it out. It involves seeking God earnestly for the pur-

21 ATTRIBUTES THAT GOD WILL REWARD

pose of knowing Him more and more. When you begin to live like that, seeking God and desiring to know Him beyond your current level of knowledge about Him, you will begin to attract divine rewards which primarily has to do with you being filled.

Become hungry and thirsty for righteousness; not only will you be filled, you will also be blessed in all you do.

Let's read that same Matthew 5:6 in two different translations; *Contemporary English Version and Good News Translation.*

'God blesses those people who want to obey him more than to eat or drink. They will be given what they want!' (CEV).

"Happy are those whose greatest desire is to do what God requires; God will satisfy them fully!" (GNT).

From these renditions, you can expect to be satisfied fully if only you will make hunger and thirst for righteousness your priority. That's one reward you sure don't want to miss.

Attribute #13

Faithfulness

"He that is faithful in that which is least is faithful also in much: and he that is unjust in the least is unjust also in much. If therefore ye have not been faithful in the unrighteous mammon, who will commit to your trust the true riches? And if ye have not been faithful in that which is another man's, who shall give you that which is your own?" (Luke 16:10-12 KJV)

A dictionary has defined faithfulness as the concept of unfailingly remaining loyal to someone or something, and putting that loyalty into consistent practice regardless of extenuating circumstances.

Faithfulness is continuing in your absolute

commitment to God even when circumstances are not favorable. There are several examples in the Bible regarding this.

For instance, Joseph had terrible ordeals while growing up – he was hated by his own brothers, sold into slavery, tempted by his master's wife, falsely accused and unjustly thrown into jail, forgotten by someone who should have helped him etc, yet He never turned his back on God. He kept serving Him and did not defile himself. He went through rough situations that anyone would describe as God's silent moment, yet He kept living as if God was looking at him because in actual fact He was looking at him. He remained loyal to God in the face of his adversity and God rewarded him handsomely by making him a ruler in a foreign country, the then world power (Genesis 37-41).

Daniel was another man who demonstrated faithfulness when he was in Babylon as a captive. There's nothing interesting and pleasurable about captivity; it was a tough experience. He was subjected to certain rules and practices he wasn't used to, yet he remained loyal to the God of Israel (despite being in Babylon). He never conformed to the land's idolatry practices despite the pressure. He refused to eat defiled meals, he prayed to God even when it meant throwing him to the lions as a consequence. He never lost sight of His God for once, even while in a strange land; and God promoted him in that land, made him wiser than his colleagues, gave him an excellent spirit and turned him into a man kings consult before making decisions. He became so great that royalty required his wisdom to rule (Daniel 1-12).

To be faithful wherever God has placed you, you must be consciously aware that He sees everything and knows everything. Every time we are at a crossroad, He is watching to see if we will compromise or remain loyal. When we have opportunity to steal with no one watching, He wants to see if we will remember Him and refrain . God is more interested in our faithfulness than our performance. He wants you to get to a level where He can confidently trust you. He told Satan that He knew Job wouldn't curse Him or compromise his commitment to him. The devil tried all he could, but Job remained steadfast and God rewarded him by restoring all he lost in double folds except for his sons and daughters (Job 1-42).

Did you know that on the last day, eternal rewards are going to be based on faithfulness? Faithful use of our gifts, talents, time, abilities, positions, potentials etc. Jesus said the faithful will be welcomed in Heaven with the following words *"Well done, thou good and faithful servant: thou hast been faithful over a few things, I will make thee ruler over many things: enter thou into the joy of thy lord."* (Matthew 25:21 KJV).

So what has God committed into your hands? Be faithful with it and you will not miss your rewards.

Attribute #14

Gratitude

"And it came to pass, as he went to Jerusalem, that he passed through the midst of Samaria and Galilee. And as he entered into a certain village, there met him ten men that were lepers, which stood afar off: And they lifted up their voices, and said, Jesus, Master, have mercy on us. And when he saw them, he said unto them, Go shew yourselves unto the priests. And it came to pass, that, as they went, they were cleansed. And one of them, when he saw that he was healed, turned back, and with a loud voice glorified God, And fell down on his face at his feet, giving him thanks: and he was a Samaritan. And Jesus answering said, Were there not ten cleansed? but where are the nine? There are not found that returned to give glory to God, save this stranger. And he said unto him, Arise, go thy way:

thy faith hath made thee whole." (Luke 17:11-19 KJV)

Jesus healed ten lepers, but only one came back to give Him thanks. The other nine went their ways as if their healing was by their own power.

Gratitude is the quality of being thankful or appreciative for kindness or benevolent gesture shown to one. 1 Thessalonians 5:18 NLT says *"Be thankful in all circumstances, for this is God's will for you who belong to Christ Jesus."*

This scripture is not written for everyone, it is written for those who are in Christ Jesus. That's why it says *'this is God's will for you'* not for everyone. So everyone around you may not be grateful, but as far as you are concerned, it is God's will for you to be thankful. Gratitude is a personal matter, not collective. In Psalm 34:1, David said *'I will bless the Lord at all times...'* He didn't say we will bless the Lord at all times. So it's a decision you will have to make regardless of what anyone around you is doing.

Why should you be grateful? Aside the fact that it is God's will concerning you, it's because He expects it according to Luke 17:17-18. Also, according to 1 Corinthians 13:9a, it's because we only know in part; we don't always know the whole story.

To enjoy the rewards of gratitude, you must start focusing on thanking God for all you have and all He makes you enjoy. You must take your attention away from the things you don't have or wish you had, as thinking about those things bring about complaining, murmuring, grumbling, comparison-based envy among other unhealthy attitudes.

Now, there is one main danger of ingratitude that I saw in the Word of God, it's in Psalm 28:5 KJV; it says: *"Because they do not regard the works of the LORD, Nor the operation of His hands, He shall destroy them And not build them* up."

Anything you are not grateful for, you are

bound to lose. It's a law! If you are not grateful for your health, expect sickness; if you are not grateful for your job, expect unemployment, if you are not grateful for God's provision, expect lack etc. And you know what? God is the one Who will do the destroying, not the devil.

So it's a very dangerous thing to be ungrateful.

Determine to live a life of gratitude beginning from now, and the rewards of gratitude will start finding their ways into your life.

Attribute #15

Godly Jealousy

"Behold, one of the children of Israel came and brought to his brothers a Midianite woman in the sight of Moses, and in the sight of all the congregation of the children of Israel, while they were weeping at the door of the Tent of Meeting. When Phinehas, the son of Eleazar, the son of Aaron the priest, saw it, he rose up from the midst of the congregation, and took a spear in his hand; and he went after the man of Israel into the pavilion, and thrust both of them through, the man of Israel, and the woman through her body. So the plague was stayed from the children of Israel. Those who died by the plague were twenty-four thousand.

Yahweh spoke to Moses, saying, Phinehas, the son of Eleazar, the son of Aaron the priest, has turned my wrath away from the children of Israel, in that he was jealous with my jealousy among them, so that I didn't consume the children of Israel in my jealousy. Therefore say, 'Behold, I give to him my covenant of peace: and it shall be to him, and to his seed after him, the covenant of an everlasting priesthood; because he was jealous for his God, and made atonement for the children of Israel.'" (Numbers 25:6-13 WEB)

Godly jealousy means defending God's interest against people or situations that seek to undermine such interests. Standing up for God's righteous cause in an environment where sin is the order of the day and also speaking up against such unrighteous living qualifies you as someone who is exhibiting godly jealousy.

Elijah stood up against Baal worship in Israel and did his best to turn the people towards the worship of Jehovah because he was jealous for His God.

Also, Phinehas in the text above demonstrated

godly jealousy when he killed some people who were committing sin while the Lord was punishing the entire nation for the sin they had already committed. The nation was almost in a mournful state by reason of the plague the Lord had sent against them because of their sins when Cozbi and Zimri were having carnal knowledge of each other right in the camp.

As a result of this act of Phinehas, the Lord put an end to the plague that was already ravaging them and rewarded Phinehas by giving him His covenant of peace and everlasting priesthood.

How jealous are you for your God? Do you defend the integrity of God's Word when mockers seek to blaspheme His Holy Word?

God rewards people who jealously protect His interests.

Attribute #16

Forgiving Others

"Therefore I say unto you, What things soever ye desire, when ye pray, believe that ye receive them, and ye shall have them. And when ye stand praying, forgive, if ye have ought against any: that your Father also which is in heaven may forgive you your trespasses. But if ye do not forgive, neither will your Father which is in heaven forgive your trespasses." (Mark 11:24-26 KJV)

Forgiveness benefits the forgiver more than the forgiven. If you don't forgive your offenders, there is no way you are going to obtain forgiveness from God. While teaching His disciples how to pray, Jesus told them to say *'forgive us our trespasses as we forgive those who trespass against us'*.

So, in order to keep receiving forgiveness from the Almighty God Who has the power to kill and make alive, you must keep forgiving others when they wrong you. You must never plan to revenge or keep grudges against your offender(s). You are to forgive just as God through Christ forgave you.

Jesus gave a parable in Matthew 18:21-35 NASB to establish this fact. It reads:

"Then Peter came and said to Him, "Lord, how often shall my brother sin against me and I forgive him? Up to seven times?" Jesus said to him, "I do not say to you, up to seven times, but up to seventy times seven.

"For this reason the kingdom of heaven may be compared to a king who wished to settle accounts with his slaves. "When he had begun to settle them, one who owed him ten thousand talents was brought to him. "But since he did not have the means to repay, his lord commanded him to be sold, along with his wife and children and all that he had, and repayment to be made. "So the slave fell to the ground and prostrated himself before him, saying, 'Have patience with me and I will repay you

everything.' "And the lord of that slave felt compassion and released him and forgave him the debt. "But that slave went out and found one of his fellow slaves who owed him a hundred denarii; and he seized him and began to choke him, saying, 'Pay back what you owe.' "So his fellow slave fell to the ground and began to plead with him, saying, 'Have patience with me and I will repay you.' "But he was unwilling and went and threw him in prison until he should pay back what was owed. "So when his fellow slaves saw what had happened, they were deeply grieved and came and reported to their lord all that had happened. "Then summoning him, his lord said to him, 'You wicked slave, I forgave you all that debt because you pleaded with me. 'Should you not also have had mercy on your fellow slave, in the same way that I had mercy on you?' "And his lord, moved with anger, handed him over to the torturers until he should repay all that was owed him. "My heavenly Father will also do the same to you, if each of you does not forgive his brother from your heart."

From this parable you can see that to deny your offenders forgiveness is to consciously invite the ministry of the tormentors. And I pray that will not be your portion in Jesus' Name.

Who do you need to forgive now? Go ahead and forgive them. Your reward will compensate for any pain you may experience in the process.

Attribute #17

Humility and Meekness

"The meek will he guide in judgment: and the meek will he teach his way." (Psalm 25:9 KJV)

"And he gives grace generously. As the Scriptures say, "God opposes the proud but gives grace to the humble." (James 4:6 NLT)

According to a dictionary, to be meek is to be humbly submissive; a quality of being humble and lowly in heart. It can also be described as having enormous power to influence situations to one's advantage or hurt someone but not using it by exercising great restraint. Jesus Christ is the first example that comes to mind as far as this subject of meekness is concerned.

Take a look at Philippians 2:5-11 NASB.

"Have this attitude in yourselves which was also in Christ Jesus, who, although He existed in the form of God, did not regard equality with God a thing to be grasped, but emptied Himself, taking the form of a bond-servant, and being made in the likeness of men. Being found in appearance as a man, He humbled Himself by becoming obedient to the point of death, even death on a cross. For this reason also, God highly exalted Him, and bestowed on Him the name which is above every name, so that at the name of Jesus every knee will bow, of those who are in heaven and on earth and under the earth, and that every tongue will confess that Jesus Christ is Lord, to the glory of God the Father."

While on earth, Jesus Christ was actually God in human form with all the power of divinity resident in Him. But because of the purpose of His coming, He decided to empty Himself of those great privileges. He humbled Himself in order to secure eternal life for all sinners.

He said something when He was about to be arrested and Peter tried to defend Him with a sword; He told Peter that He didn't need any defense. He said He could ask His Father and twelve (12) legions of angels would be sent to defend Him if He needed defense (Matthew 26:53-54).

Now, a legion has been defined as a unit of 3,000 – 6,000 men in the ancient Roman army. So twelve (12) legions of angels would mean 36,000 – 72,000 angels at the very least.

If you check 2 Kings 19:35, one angel attacked the camp of the Assyrians and killed 185,000 soldiers in one night. So, if one angel has the capacity to kill 185,000 people in just one night, how many do you think 12 legions (36,000 – 72,000 angels) would kill? You do the math.

Jesus had such powers, yet He allowed ordinary men to arrest and crucify Him in order to fulfill what the scriptures had said about Him. Now that's meekness in its raw form.

And if you look at Matthew 11:29 KJV, He invited us to emulate His meekness. He said:

"Take my yoke upon you, and learn of me; for I am meek and lowly in heart: and ye shall find rest unto your souls."

Meekness attracts great rewards from God because it is His own very nature.

In the course of my study, I was able to identify some rewards of meekness. If you are meek, expect the following according to the Word of God:

1. God hides you in the days of His anger – Zephaniah 2:3
2. Laws are suspended in your favour – Galatians 5:23
3. You shall eat and be satisfied – Psalm 22:26
4. You will enjoy divine guidance – Psalm 25:9

5. You shall inherit the earth and enjoy abundance of peace – Psalm 37:11; Matthew 5:5; Matthew 11:29
6. You enjoy God's salvation – Psalm 76:9
7. You enjoy divine lifting – Psalm 147:6
8. God beautifies you with salvation – Psalm 149:4
9. You enjoy divine defense –Isaiah 11:4
10. You enjoy increased joy – Isaiah 29:19
11. You enjoy good news – Isaiah 61:1
12. You enjoy high rating with God – 1 Peter 3:4.

All these and many more are the rewards you can look forward to if only you will learn from Christ and start living your life in humility and meekness.

Attribute #18

Holiness and Consecration

"Make every effort to live in peace with everyone and to be holy; without holiness no one will see the Lord." (Hebrews 12:14 NIV)

"But in a great house there are not only vessels of gold and silver, but also of wood and clay, some for honor and some for dishonor. Therefore if anyone cleanses himself from the latter, he will be a vessel for honor, sanctified and useful for the Master, prepared for every good work." (2 Timothy 2:20-21 NKJV)

In 1 Peter 1:15-16, the Lord said you have to be holy because He is holy.

What then is holiness? Simply put, it is living a consecrated life. You live your life as a living sacrifice, totally dedicated and devoted to God. To live holy is to live your life in absolute accordance with the Word of God.

But before this, that Hebrews 12:14 says you should make every effort to live in peace with everyone. That part is also very important. As a matter of fact, it came first in that verse. The Lord wants you to be at peace with yourself, your spouse, your children, your parents, your friends, and even your enemies. He said *'with everyone'* no exception.

So you must live a peaceful life and a holy life to be able to see the Lord and in order to become a vessel unto honour, suitable for His honorable use.

According to 2 Timothy 2:20-21 quoted above, you will need to cleanse yourself from anything that defiles – sin, bad habits, wrong relationships, anger, malice etc. You must be totally sanctified (separated) unto the Lord for a life of Kingdom impact.

Attribute #19

Godly Marriage

*"Behold, children are a heritage from the Lord,
The fruit of the womb is a reward.
Like arrows in the hand of a warrior, So are the children of one's youth.*

Happy is the man who has his quiver full of them;
They shall not be ashamed, But shall speak with their enemies in the gate." (Psalm 127:3-5 NKJV)

"But did He not make them one, Having a remnant of the Spirit?
And why one? He seeks godly offspring.

Therefore take heed to your spirit,
And let none deal treacherously with the wife of his youth.

"For the Lord God of Israel says That He

hates divorce,
For it covers one's garment with violence," Says the Lord of hosts.

"Therefore take heed to your spirit, That you do not deal treacherously." (Malachi 2:15-16 NKJV)

Take a good look at these scriptures; one main reason the Lord hates divorce and delights in marriages is because He seeks godly seeds. He has wonderful children to release into the world for His great purposes, but He doesn't just send them anyhow. He looks for godly marriages and blesses them with His reward – Fruits of the Womb.

That's one way God rewards married couples who are faithful to one another and to the vows they took in His Presence. He blesses them with godly children.

So, how is your marriage working out? Ensure you remain faithful and committed to your spouse, and don't entertain the thought of divorce for a moment; your reward is going to be very great.

Attribute #20

Righteous Living

"Whoever pursues righteousness and love finds life, prosperity and honor." (Proverbs 21:21 NIV)

"Gray hair is a crown of splendor; it is attained in the way of righteousness." (Proverbs 16:31 NIV)

The Word of God says living a righteous life has the capacity to attract prosperity and honour to you. And this is very true. You remember Matthew 6:33? It says if you seek the Kingdom of God and His righteousness as your priority, every other thing including prosperity and honour will be added to you.

In addition to that, the Bible says gray hair is a crown of splendor and it is attained in the way of righteousness. You know what that means? It means to live a righteous life is to technically avoid untimely death. It means there is a relationship between righteous living and longevity, hence the gray hair.

So when you decide to live a righteous life before the Lord, you are the one actually benefitting, not Him.

Righteous living yields earthly rewards and also yields eternal ones. It's a life worth living.

Attribute #21

Persecution

"God blesses you when people mock you and persecute you and lie about you and say all sorts of evil things against you because you are my followers. Be happy about it! Be very glad! For a great reward awaits you in heaven. And remember, the ancient prophets were persecuted in the same way." (Matthew 5:11-12 NLT)

Jesus did not hide this truth from His disciples then, and even now He is still pointing our attention to it. Persecution is part of the Gospel package.

He said in John 15:20 ESV *"Remember the word that I said to you: 'A servant is not greater than his master.' If they persecuted me, they will also per-*

secute you. If they kept my word, they will also keep yours."

If Jesus Christ and His early followers couldn't escape persecution, it definitely will come to you at one point or the other.

A dictionary has described persecution as subjecting (someone) to hostility and ill-treatment, especially because of their race or political or religious beliefs. In this case, persecution comes to you as a result of your faith in Jesus Christ and His work of salvation on the cross.

Just because you believe in Jesus Christ, you might face some forms of persecution in your place of work, school, community, society or even in your family. People may start maltreating you, spreading false rumours about you or even inflict injuries on you.

Jesus said you should be happy about such treatments because a great reward awaits you in heaven. Pray for your persecutors (Matthew

5:44-46) and be thankful for the opportunity to qualify for the reward reserved for the persecuted (Acts 5:40-41).

2 Timothy 3:12 KJV says *"...all that will live godly in Christ Jesus shall suffer persecution."*

You know what that means? It means the moment you decided to accept Jesus Christ as your Lord and Saviour and also decided to live for Him, you automatically signed up for persecution.

So just keep living your life for Jesus; endure any persecution that comes your way and rejoice because great is your reward in heaven.

Conclusion

In the course of this book, the Lord has opened our eyes to 21 Attributes that will attract His reward every time. The purpose is not just to know, document or preach them, rather they were revealed so that we can walk in them; so that we can begin to enjoy His rewards in every area of our lives.

Can the integrity of God be depended upon to expect these rewards? Yes, of course. How can we be so sure? Well, He sees, hears and knows all things including our motives; He's just and as a result cannot be bribed because He is not corrupt; He's unlimited in resources and as such can afford anything no matter how big; He is sovereign so no man can question Him and lastly, He has a proven track record of rewarding others (Genesis 15:1).

21 ATTRIBUTES THAT GOD WILL REWARD

According to John 8:32, only the truth that is known sets free. Go over these attributes one by one and determine to build up your life around them.

Jesus said in John 13:17(NLT) - *"You know these things- now do them! That is the path of blessing."*

As you determine to begin to live out these attributes on a daily basis, may the Lord shine His light into every area of your life and cause your rewards to locate you speedily in Jesus' Name.

WHY YOU REALLY NEED JESUS!

You might have heard a lot of Preachers talk about the importance of surrendering one's life to Jesus and even the dangers of not doing so at one time or the other without you being really moved. But with these three (3) important reasons highlighted below, I strongly believe you will not need another sermon before deciding to yield to His saving grace regardless of your religious beliefs.

1. **You have an Enemy to overcome:** There is an adversary who is all out to steal from you, kill you and destroy you regardless of your level of education, moral uprightness, societal influence or even religious beliefs. He is Devil by name (John 10:10, 1 Peter 5: 8), and he doesn't release any of

his captives until he completely destroys their souls in hell. The ONLY One Who can deliver you from his manipulations and also save your soul from him is Jesus Christ.

2. **You have an Appointment to keep:** Being alive and reading this implies you have a very important and inevitable appointment to keep. It is an appointment with death (Hebrews 9:27). Death is the sure end of all mortals (of which you are part); and to enable you prepare for this appointment without fear of eternal damnation, you need Jesus. He is the ONLY One Who has power over death (Revelation 1:18).

3. **You have a Judge to face:** Upon departure from this earth, you will have to stand before a judgment throne to render an account of your earthly life (Hebrews 9:27, Romans 14:12). The outcome of this judgment is what will determine your eternal abode which will either be Heaven

or the Lake of fire. Interestingly, the Judge Who will preside over your case and also decide where you will spend your eternity is Jesus (John 5:21-30, 2 Timothy 4:1). I perceive you are thinking "is God not our Judge? Why Jesus?' Well, you are not wrong. But God the Father Himself is the One Who handed over all the judgment to His Son, Jesus Christ. Read the verse 22 of that John chapter 5. So Jesus is the ONLY One Who has the power to either judge you guilty or guiltless in eternity.

Now that you know these, the wisest thing you can do for yourself is to quickly establish a relationship with Jesus, since you don't even know how close your appointment with death is. To do this, say this prayer aloud:

"Lord Jesus, I am a sinner and I cannot help myself. Wash me in your precious blood and make me a new creature. I open the door of my heart to you today, come into my life and become my Lord and Savior. Grant me the grace

to overcome the devil, prepare me for eternity and help me to escape the judgment reserved for sinners. Thank You Jesus for saving me. Amen."

Congratulations! You are now SAVED. Go and sin no more.

To learn more about your new relationship with Jesus, kindly send an Email to info@gloem.org or emancipation4souls@yahoo.com, we will send you a material that will help you. You can also call, text or send whatsapp message to +1 587 9735910 or +1 587 9695910 for further assistance.

And to learn more about God, His Word and His plans for your life, kindly visit our Facebook page [*https://www.facebook.com/gloem.org*] for daily meditation in the Word of God (all year round) and our Blog page [*https://gloem.org/my-blog*] for life transforming publications.

You are also invited to listen to Freedom Podcast: The Official Weekly Podcast of Global Emancipation Ministries – Calgary via https://anchor.fm/gloem

All these great resources capable of developing your spiritual stamina will help you become an overcomer in life regardless of what comes your way.

PRAYER POINTS

1. Father, thank You for opening my eyes to the truths contained in this book.
2. Father, please cause all my expectations to come to pass speedily.
3. I cancel everything hindering answers to my prayers in Jesus' Name.
4. God of all possibilities, please cause my grass to become green again.
5. From today, my breakthrough shall no longer be delayed in Jesus' Name.
6. Father, beginning from now, please release upon me and my household the ability to walk with you faithfully in the Name of Jesus.
7. Father, I thank You for answering all my prayers. Glory be to Your Holy Name. Hallelujah!

BECOME A FINANCIAL PARTNER WITH JESUS

At ***Global Emancipation Ministries - Calgary***, our mandate is ***to liberate men through the knowledge of the Truth*** and our mission statement is ***creating channels through which men can encounter the Truth - [Isaiah 61:1-3; John 8:32, 36; I Thessalonians 5:24].***

Our Ministerial Activities include Rural and Urban Evangelical Outreaches, Prison Evangelism, Hospital Ministrations, Mobilization for Missions Support, Teaching of the undiluted Word of God, Scripture-Based Seminars, Discipleship, Training of Field Missionaries and Empowerment of underprivileged ones among other Field Ministerial Tasks.

If you sense the Lord is calling you to reach out to the lost by engaging in any of these activities or by assisting those involved with your resources, please feel free to join us. Let us come together as we take the Gospel of our Lord Jesus Christ to the hurting and forgotten ones. [Mark 16:15-20].

Please join us in these kingdom projects by making your weekly, monthly, quarterly or annual donations to Global Emancipation Ministries – Calgary.

You can visit the "GIVE" section on our website, www.gloem.org, to learn about the ways to give.

For acknowledgement, please advise your donations to us by email: info@gloem.org or emancipation4souls@yahoo.com, and kindly include your details i.e. name, address, email and location. Alternatively, you can simply call +1 587 9735910 to do same.

-

You can also volunteer your gifts and talents in the service of the Lord through our ministerial platforms regardless of your location. To get information on how to go about this, please visit www.gloem.org and contact us via email: info@gloem.org or emancipation4souls@yahoo.com.

God bless you.

About the Author

By the special grace of God, **Anthony O. Adefarakan** is the privileged President of **Global Emancipation Ministries - Calgary (GLOEM)** with headquarters in Canada, North America and **Emancipating Truth Ministry International (ETMI)** with headquarters in Nigeria, West Africa.

The Lord called him into the field ministry in February 2008 with the mandate to liberate men through the knowledge of the Truth, and by December 2012 he was ordained and commissioned as the Pioneer Pastor – in – Charge of The Redeemed Christian Church of God, Revelation Parish, Shalom Area under Delta Province III, Nigeria where he served until 1st February 2015 when he officially handed over to a new Pastor in order to focus on his field ministry to which the Lord had earlier called him and for which the authority of the church had already prayed and released him to undertake.

On 29th September 2013, he was awarded a Post Graduate Diploma in Tent – Making Mission from the Redeemed Christian School of Missions, Nigeria (RECSOM, Asaba Campus) where he also had the privilege to train Pastors and Missionaries as a lecturer in 2017.

Since the commissioning of his field ministry in 2015 he has had the opportunity to lead his ministry officers to field ministrations in different Prisons, Hospitals, Orphanages, Rural communities, Camp settlements, Markets, Local churches among other places with great successes on all occasions – such as salvation of sinners, healing of the sick, financial empowerment of mission churches, provision of relief materials to the poor, provision of medical services to the underprivileged, baptism in the Holy Ghost, deliverance from demonic oppression, release of inmates just to mention a few - all to the glory of God Who alone is the Doer.

He is the author of other best-selling titles such as *The Law of Kinds, Learning From the Ants, The Immutability of God's Counsel, Surely there is an End, Life Applicable lessons from the Book of Ruth, One thing is Needful Weekly Devotional Guide, Life Applicable Revelations from God's Word* (Volumes 1 and 2) among others.

He is blissfully married to Ifeoluwa A. Adefarakan and their marriage is fruitful to the glory of God.

Jesus is his Message, Freedom is the Outcome!
Isaiah 61:1-3

www.ingramcontent.com/pod-product-compliance
Lightning Source LLC
Chambersburg PA
CBHW021429070526
44577CB00001B/122